EMPOWERED
2022

WHISPERS ON THE WIND

Edited By Donna Samworth

First published in Great Britain in 2022 by:

YoungWriters
Est. 1991

Young Writers
Remus House
Coltsfoot Drive
Peterborough
PE2 9BF
Telephone: 01733 890066
Website: www.youngwriters.co.uk

Book Design by Ashley Janson

Softback ISBN 978-1-80015-311-0

Printed and bound in the UK by BookPrintingUK
Website: www.bookprintinguk.com
YB0517E

☆ FOREWORD ☆

Since 1991, here at Young Writers we have celebrated the awesome power of creative writing, especially in young adults where it can serve as a vital method of expressing their emotions and views about the world around them. In every poem we see the effort and thought that each student published in this book has put into their work and by creating this anthology we hope to encourage them further with the ultimate goal of sparking a life-long love of writing.

Our latest competition for secondary school students, Empowered, challenged young writers to consider what was important to them. We wanted to give them a voice, the chance to express themselves freely and honestly, something which is so important for these young adults to feel confident and listened to. They could give an opinion, share a memory, consider a dilemma, impart advice or simply write about something they love. There were no restrictions on style or subject so you will find an anthology brimming with a variety of poetic styles and topics. We hope you find it as absorbing as we have.

We encourage young writers to express themselves and address subjects that matter to them, which sometimes means writing about sensitive or contentious topics. If you have been affected by any issues raised in this book, details on where to find help can be found at www.youngwriters.co.uk/info/other/contact-lines

✯ CONTENTS ✯

THE POEMS

Time Tells

This world has changed over time and time
Our generation and style, so has mine
So cold, so silent the time goes quick
An hour to a year so make the most of it

Back in the past, it never went so fast
It was like a clock that would always last
No computers, no phones, no one would be alone
Everyone would have fun playing in the sun

I wish, I want to go back in time
To see little girls singing in rhyme
Playing street games and running around
Where horses would gallop and shake the ground

The whistle of steam trains is an old, lost sound
Compared to the modern day where everyone is bustling around
From carriages to cars, from books to tablets
I wish this time would never change.

Penelope Jones (11)
Ash Green School, Ash Green

Transgender

Born in one body, longing for another
Cursed to depression, seemingly forever
Oppressed and bullied for the creator's mistake
We sit and smile until we break
'Not real' this and 'faker' that
He's too thin and she's too fat!
She's too tall and he's too short
We feel trapped, we feel caught
Lying on our own personal hells
Forced to be bullied or end ourselves
The brave ones push through and are proud of their scars
The strongest ones with the largest hearts
We honour our fallen by carrying on
And eventually the battle will be won.

Evie Whiteside (14)
Ash Green School, Ash Green

Who Do I Want To Be?

Who could I be?
What is my future?
I think about it every night
Who could I be?

Singers, swimmers and skiers
The empowering thought takes over me
Diver or designer
Who do I want to be?

I see my idols be successful
Maybe I'll be like them one day too
I can work hard and work my way up
What could I do?

I dream and dream and hope for more
And maybe I could be successful in 2034
But I have to work and dream like my idols
To complete my ambition, hopes and dreams.

Laura Chung (12)
Ash Green School, Ash Green

My Marvellous Mum

My mum inspires me
Encouraging me from day one
Inspiring me to do everything I've ever done
She is exactly like Superwoman

Always being there for me
When I need her
Working hard 24/7
To provide for her family

A prodigious person she is
She doesn't expect anything in return
For everything she gives
She is the most sympathetic person ever

Always standing up for me
At the toughest times
I know I can tell her anything and everything
I love her so much.

Anya Jagotta (12)
Ash Green School, Ash Green

Finding Myself

Is there anyone there
To help me see
Help me remember
Remember to be me?
For I feel like now
I am someone else
And I need help
To find myself
Sometimes my thoughts might drift away
With the empty look, it might portray
You think I'm doing nothing but I'm doing my best
To put my busy mind to rest
Always so tired, trying to find the strength
And keep my loved ones at arm's length
Neer wanting my family to see a once happy woman
Is now me.

Bethany Perry (14)
Ash Green School, Ash Green

Mirror, Mirror On The Wall

When she looked at the mirror
She couldn't help but cry
When she tried to cover up
They couldn't help but sigh

When he looked at his friends
He tried not to hide
Happiness in himself
He couldn't seem to find

She was tired
Of not feeling proud
He was tired
Of not speaking out

But in reality
They were beautiful in their own way
Beautiful
Was all they needed someone to say.

Parneet Kaur (12)
Ash Green School, Ash Green

Imagination Stories

The place where imagination is set wild
Let all the thoughts flow free
Words dancing on a page
Some characters happy, some filled with rage

Heroes and villains always brawling
Bad guys always end up falling
Books for kids, books that are gory
Books are imagination stories

Writing feels like being set free
Fills you up with glee
Feeling different emotions
Writing is an empowered potion.

Aman Khala (12)
Ash Green School, Ash Green

Destruction Within Our World

Our world is precious
Beyond compare
It will never go
But that isn't a promise

Destruction is happiness as we speak
Trees are like falling dominoes
Pollution has suffocated us

The sky is a black hole
Trees are bare and brown
Nature is missing

So believe in what you stand for
Do what's right
So we can find some light.

Manroop Sandhu (12)
Ash Green School, Ash Green

Road To Goals

How football makes me feel
It makes me feel like I am dancing on clouds
Them 90 minutes make me feel at home
One day I'll be on the big screen

Whilst I'm on that big screen
I know I'll make people happy
And I will thank everyone who taught me anything

I just wish they were all still here
So one day they could see me once again.

Brendan Davies (12)
Ash Green School, Ash Green

Crochet Hope

A hook in a ball of yarn
Twisting and turning
Making imagination become reality
Don't give up!

Masterpieces coming together
As if they are a pack of animals
Don't give up

At the end of the day
Everything was formed like clay
Creating dreamlife
If you believe in your dreams
They will come true
Never give up!

Mya Bhoohe (12)
Ash Green School, Ash Green

Let's Save The Planet

Do you even care about this world we share
If we continue one day it will be bare
Because our world is dying
But all you grown-ups think we are lying
We are polluting the atmosphere
And one day we may need to move to the stratosphere
All life will go extinct
Unless we follow this instinct
Let's stop this habit
Let's save the planet.

Cory Marsh (13)
Ash Green School, Ash Green

Save The Endangered

Sea levels rise
Polar bears cry
The ice melts
The polar bears sigh

We litter
The turtles suffer
Their lives get rougher
While we litter

The pandas eat
You lie
They die
They fly high

The pollution you cause
Harms them
When you litter
You harm them.
Save the endangered

Yasmin Mann (12)
Ash Green School, Ash Green

Chaos In Ukraine

Ukraine doesn't have a chance
Russia's gone too far
The defence is going down
It's all just a disaster

People are dying
The city's destroyed
Everyone's begging
But Putin won't stop

Kyiv is demolished
Zelenskyy is mad
The war is bad
And Putin won't stop!

Kevin Tung (12)
Ash Green School, Ash Green

Save The Turtles

Save the turtles
Day and night
I'm constantly dodging the murderers
Now my situation is do or die

Save the turtles
If I ever get tricked
I'll have to sleep tight
And say goodbye

Save the turtles
I'm trapped
It's time to turn out the light
Let's say goodnight.

Mandy-Joyce Millet (11)
Ash Green School, Ash Green

Gymnastics

I love you, I hate you
After all we have been through
The pain and suffering you have caused
The happiness and joy and applause
Every new skill learnt and completed
Another competition proudly competed.

Grace Bohdanowitsch (14)
Ash Green School, Ash Green

The Environment

Sea levels rise
The polar bear cries
The ice drips
Temperature's high

The panda yelps
Crying for help
His family dead
While he was lying in his bed.

Evie Austerberry (11)
Ash Green School, Ash Green

Do You Know What Education Is All About?

Education is important for us to learn
It is the way of understanding how the world turns
But it is always better to feel awake
Because school can be hard but you will be okay
Education is important for us to learn
It gives us confidence and options without delay
But others believe that they are confident anyway
Because we can fit in if we do things okay
Education is important for us to learn
Opportunities are a great help for us to earn
Lots of money, experience and inspiration
Because lots of people need a little help some days
Education is important for us to learn
It's a way to gain some trustful social skills
So you can interact with others and make a few friends.

James Moreland (13)
Cansfield High School, Ashton-In-Makerfield

Education

Education
Something I have always yearned for
How fortunate are they that they have such an opportunity
As they say: 'knowledge is power'
I would have so many opportunities
A future so bright, I would have no worries
I won't have to worry about money
The things I would do to have an education
Oh how lucky are they?

They say good things come to those who deserve them
But what wrong have I done to deserve such a fate?
A fate so cruel
It robbed me of a chance at education
Oh how lucky are they?

Maxine Chioto (15)
Cansfield High School, Ashton-In-Makerfield

Education

E xcellence - what everyone aims for
D ynamic - how everyone needs to feel
U nbelievable - how much amazing work there is
C ourage - this is one of the keys to success
A wesomeness - this is what your work is like
T errific - your potential
I nteresting - all lessons have this in common
O pportunity - there are thousands at the tip of your fingers
N ationwide - everyone can achieve something.

Jonathan Grundy (12)
Cansfield High School, Ashton-In-Makerfield

Dear Young Me

Dear young me
I wish I could have confidence
I wish I was not scared to stand up for myself

Dear young me
I wish I was not afraid to speak up
I wish I was not scared to be the real me

Dear young me
I wish I did not care what people thought about me

Dear young me
I wish that I did not waste time worrying about ageing
And lived in the moment.

Isabelle Nisbet (13)
Cansfield High School, Ashton-In-Makerfield

Mysterious Waterfall

The sound of the wind whistling against the lonely tall tree
The melodies of the glorious bluebird chirping is oh so sweet
A waterfall deep in the forest glistening so bright and oh so wonderful
The tiny droplets of heavenly water fill whose cup?
The burning heat from the bold sun surrounds the rainforest
The damp hot feeling from the trees
The sweat dripping from one's face
The ring of a finger shining like diamonds
The mist fills the air
Colourful tribes hunt for their enemies
The sound of tropical flutes being played in the distance
Someone waits for the magnificent mango sunset
The sky clears
Darkness falls
A hungry lion roars
Ships await their captains
Who knows what will happen
The rainforest has emotions no one can notice.

M A (14)
Chase House School, Brownhills

Until I Am A Survivor

It comes in all different shapes and sizes
It doesn't care who you are and who you want to be
It takes it moment to shine and take yours away
It makes you cold, ill and numb
It makes you wish it will all go away
It doesn't just go away on Christmas Day or any other special day
It makes you feel like nothing will ever be right again
And all of your hopes and dreams just blow away
But it doesn't change that you are loved more than anyone will know
And maybe even one day you will shout you survived but will save that for another day
And if you make it, you will dance the night away
And if don't make it for one more day, it will all be okay
But for now you will take it day by day until everything is okay.

T S (13)
Chase House School, Brownhills

Hopes And Dreams

Hopes and dreams can come true
If you work hard your dream becomes real
You don't have to sit and hope it will peel
I want a job, a car and a house
Living my dream, not as a mouse
Cats and dogs will make me happy
Jumping around with my little chappy
My hopes and dreams will come true
I work hard all day through
Makes me who we really are.

C S (13)
Chase House School, Brownhills

The Environment

Don't throw your litter
Put it in the bin
Plastic bottles can be a sin
Plastic bags we now reuse
Because we are cool dudes
Care for the environment and its creatures
Be an environment reacher
Moving forward like a snake
Don't just throw your unwanted cake
Save the environment and be cool
Don't be a bin dodger, be cool.

L W (14)
Chase House School, Brownhills

No More

I see them drilling for oil with their colossal machines of
destruction. Straight through the earth, drilling and drilling.
I screech, "No more!"

I see them hacking away at the trees. These trees took
hundreds of years to grow, and just like that, they're dead.
I screech, "No more!"

I see them laughing as they throw plastic waste into the
river, oblivious to the fact that there are fish in that river,
about to choke on the pieces of plastic left behind.
I screech, "No more!"

I see them shoot at the Earth's innocent creatures, just
because they're worth some money. Bears, foxes, wolves -
all killed for their coats.
I screech, "No more!"

I see them dump petrol in the ocean because they can't be
bothered to safely dispose of it, unaware that they are
poisoning sea creatures.
I screech, "No more!"

I see them set fire to the soul of the Earth.
I screech, "No more!"

I screech and screech, but my cries of despair fall upon deaf
ears. The world is dying - and there's nothing I can do.

Grace Jones (14)
Cheadle Hulme High School, Cheadle Hulme

The Wand In My Attic

I found a wand in my attic
I don't know where it came from or how it came to be
My mum and dad are clueless about it
But when I touch it, feel the power
To topple every evil tower

This wand is powerful
There is no doubt
Of that much I am sure
Question is though
How am I going to use it?

I could silence every bully, who called anyone names
'Freak', 'weirdo' and 'screwball'
With a simple wave of my wand
I could silence them all
Stop the hurtful waterfall

I could stop those who would do harm to others
The racism, sexism, homophobia
And all the other names of pain
A better world for all
Where all could walk hand in hand

I could end wars and battles
Topple the walls
End the lives of those who stole the happiness of others
And still claim to be a force for good
The roars of tyrants forever silenced

I could save the world
From climate change, logging and poaching
Save every animal; polar bear and pangolin alike
I could repair the ozone layer
And let everyone breathe

I could extend humanity's limits
To stretch our grasp around the universe
We could rule the void and
Receive a medal from Elon
Without even breaking a sweat

I could stop the atrocities and tragedies and more
Stop all the pain and hate
Before it's all too late
And no one would hold it against me
If I had to kill a few despot rulers

But then I stop
And sadly laugh and grin
Because if I did all that I say I will
It will have been for naught
Because the humanity will never learn

So I smile
A melancholy smile nonetheless
I know I would be corrupted
Like the dictators, whose countries I would have liberated
Because I am not perfect, and none of us are

So I leave the wand where I found it
But I then stop
What if the potential of the wand could be shared by all?
So I break the wand in two
So now the spells lie with you.

Guillermo Ortega-Ruggia (14)
Cheadle Hulme High School, Cheadle Hulme

The Delusion We Cry

Across the world, we cry
We're the most equal
Tell that to the children of Ethiopia too
The children in Ethiopia who struggle to survive day by day
Tell that to the Indian child
Who slaves away unnoticed on a factory floor
Tell that to the American child
Sprawled before the plasma TV

Across the world, we cry
We're the most liberal
Tell that to the Afghan woman
Cloaked from the world, her voice muffled
Tell that to the gay couple in Saudi Arabia
Arrested for their sexuality
Tell that to the British white man
Walking through Trafalgar Square unmolested

Across the world, we cry
We're the most accepting
Tell that to the migrant who struggles for a better life only to be turned away
Tell that to the Muslim girl in France
Shunned for what she believes in
Tell that to the Christian American
Who never seems to be ignored.

Tom Overland (14)
Cheadle Hulme High School, Cheadle Hulme

Our Sincerest Apologies

We're sorry.
We're sorry for trying to raise a world
Where flowers can grow
And children can learn
But what's the point
If there's not a world left.
Did you hear?
We have fifty years
Before the ice can't freeze
And half the animals we live with now
Can't be found.
Why do we teach about 'quadratic graphs'
I just find it daft when we
Could be learning about 'climate science'
Something that could be helpful to save
Our, dying planet.
We're told to 'go outside'
But you refuse to open your eyes
To the fact that soon,
There won't be an outside.
In the next few years
We have to make a change
Don't get me wrong
Protests, strikes, are all well and good
But if our leaders and politicians

Don't bother to listen
It's all on us.
You left this for us.
So I'm sorry. We're sorry.
Without more acceptance
That our planet is crumbling
It will be too late
We can't procrastinate
We need to change now
If it's 2070 and you're reading this,
We're so sorry that you had to miss
On all the things we used to love
Just because
We weren't listened to enough.

George Smith
Cheadle Hulme High School, Cheadle Hulme

Empowered

The strength to rise from the pain
To continue at all costs
The strength to prolong the pain
Knowing what you have lost
The strength to smile, when all you feel is anger
To substitute bad days for the best ones so you can remember
The strength to say 'I'm lost' when your pride is blocked
To say 'Please love me', though I have never done it right
The strength to say you love them, knowing there may be
To stay by their side at times, when all they do is cry
The strength to try again after many times of failing
To finally open up after many years of waiting
The strength to fall in love though sacrificing your heart
To keep a loved one close while knowing you've grown
The strength to say 'I love you' when all else has gone wrong
To keep on waiting for you regardless of how long it is.

Meshal Zulfiqar (12)
Cheadle Hulme High School, Cheadle Hulme

The Weed

All it takes is one weed
In the garden, flowers flourish
Insects live and plants grow
Living in their own ecosystem

As soon as the weed grows,
Everything changes
It grows next to the flowers
Getting bigger and bigger
Stronger and stronger

If things go untouched, unhelped
It invades
Flowers dying as it expands
Its reach of power expanding

Insects flee
Their homes destroyed
Leaving everything behind
As the weed takes control

How can the gardener let this happen,
Just stood watching and judging?
Yet there is no time for it
We need to make a stand
A stand for Ukraine
To help remove this weed.

Luke Anderton (14)
Cheadle Hulme High School, Cheadle Hulme

The Moments

There are times
When it all feels too much
When everything's to come
And you feel helpless and lost

There are moments
When everything's falling on you
When you're pressured
And you feel alone and sad

And then there are times
When you're at peace
When you're doing your favourite things
And you feel content

And there are moments
When you've done something great
When you've faced those fears
And you feel confident

And they're the best of times
When your life's at its peak
When you're just happy being you
And you feel empowered.

Chrissie Hurd (14)
Cheadle Hulme High School, Cheadle Hulme

Myself

e **M** powerment to me is myself, my dreams and hopes are high as colourful as a canvas in all glory and
Y ou my friends, precious to me, you are as amazing as life in all its glory
S ocial media is trapped. I feel as if others hide behind the screen as captivating as a cage in its dim light, our
E nvironment crumbles beneath our feet, unwell it is because of us, as delicate as glass in its dim light
L ife I value because I have the choice. It gives me wings to fly as free as a bird, my love lives on
F amily and friends will me on, they empower me. As close as sisters, my love lives on.

Emily Fox
Cheadle Hulme High School, Cheadle Hulme

Humanity

Humanity is where we grow from,
Where we make our identities,
Make our personalities.

Humanity is how we meet people,
How we can change lives,
How we live.

Humanity is what we call for,
Live for,
Hope for.

But humanity,
We don't get.

Whether you're:
Gay,
Straight,
Bisexual,
Transgender.

Humanity needs to learn,
Humanity needs equality,
Humanity needs to learn to love,
You for who *you* are.

Riley Killingbeck (14)
Cheadle Hulme High School, Cheadle Hulme

Story Of My Life

A seed from a flower I grew,
Getting taught by the parents I knew,
Since I was two.
Since I was three,
I knew how to do,
So many things,
But only a couple were true.
Since I was four,
I knew how to crawl on the floor.
Since I was five,
I felt alive.
Since I was six,
I whittled sticks.
Since I was seven,
I believed in Heaven.
That's the story of my life so far,
Not really, but you get the point.
If this was longer,
I'd be waffling.

Kingsley Mak (14)
Cheadle Hulme High School, Cheadle Hulme

A Strong Word

Empowerment is a very strong word
Empowerment is a voice that can be heard
But very few people have rights to such power
It's only the people who speak very sour
So what about the people who feel low?
They have nowhere to run and nowhere to go
Concentration camps or being a young carer
What can we do to make the world fairer?
Give them power?
But empowerment is a strong word
So let's let millions more voices now be heard.

George White (14)
Cheadle Hulme High School, Cheadle Hulme

Raise Your Voice

What is it to you?
What is it to me?
Is it to help or inspire
Or is it wishing every night?
What is it to me?
Is it to aide
Or is it to be afraid?
To have a choice?
To raise your voice?
Is it to be alone?
To frown?
Is it to be in light
And overcome the night?
To tower fears?
To ignite power?
It's your choice
Raise your voice!

Jessica Davies (14)
Cheadle Hulme High School, Cheadle Hulme

To Empower

People fall like a chart
The loss of love hits like a dart
You can only feel the pain when you depart
No one can fix the hole in your heart
Nothing feels worse than when we're apart
Alas, you have to move along and restart
Even though it may hurt at the start
You must progress past the echoing pain
To refill the gap in your heart.

Misha Rohman (11)
Cheadle Hulme High School, Cheadle Hulme

Blank Paper

The daunting desk, by which I sit,
Pen or pencil, paper plain,
I stay still stuck, trying to think,
Oh! A thought!
... It's gone again.
But prior pen pressed, in idle thought,
Passion and emotion, inspiration I find.
But vainly vanish, all for naught,
The paper is blank, empty mind.

William Cliff
Cheadle Hulme High School, Cheadle Hulme

My Own Two Hands

I want to be a writer and use my hands
To put pen to paper and create distant lands
An idea is formed and it springs onto the page
I put my mind to it and soon I'm engaged
I'm writing the next chapter, the next paragraph and line
I think of what place and what period of time
What characters will star in this story of mine?
What will come into existence in this universe, this world and these lands
That I have created with my own two hands?

Beniamin Pasierbski (13)
Christ The King Catholic Voluntary Academy, Arnold

Dear Future Me

Dear future me
I hope you did well and focussed in school
I know it was hard to pay attention
Did you get a good score for your GCSEs?
I know you were always anxious about them!

Dear future me
What are you doing career-wise?
Did you go towards being a doctor?
I know it must have been hard
But I would do anything to save lives
Like the brilliant people that saved mine.

Dear future me
Have you told your family and friends you love them?
They have been brilliant and are always by my side
Trust me if you ever need help they are the people to go to
My family will always have my heart!

Dear future me
I know you are doing great
Don't let your health condition bring you down, you are stronger
Don't let anything bring you down
You can conquer the world.

Monique Bertrand (12)
Conisborough College, Catford

Dreams To Work For

Everybody has dreams
I have dreams
You have dreams
Some people have reached their dreams
Some haven't
But dreams will only work for you if you work hard
So to reach your full potential like me
You need to get outside your comfort zone
I'll always try and work as hard as possible
This is what empowers me
You won't reach your dreams if you are always in your comfort zone
You must be vulnerable in your comfort zone
Like an alone zebra in a jungle
So you need to get comfortable being uncomfortable
If you want to make it
That's what empowers me
I'll work hard every day
So my dreams comfort me
Let's think
What are our dreams?
What do you need to achieve them?
Now let's stop plotting and wondering about what's happened in the past
Now I will work hard being me

So will you
We can do this!

Mason Jenner (12)
Conisborough College, Catford

Keep Looking Up

Life may be hard,
It will get better,
This doesn't last forever,
Give it a day,
Week,
A month,
It will change,
If you try hard enough,
Keep looking up,
You may cry in fear,
Or lie to stop tears,
You may try to leave,
Try and relive,
The pain it caused you that day,
That year,
Keep looking up,
Life is good,
If you keep the peace,
Don't let the war go on in your head,
It will affect the things I've said,
Never stop thinking,
But stop thinking,
Keep looking up,
Keep your eye on the prize,
Don't despise what people say,

It may not be your way,
You gotta keep looking forward,
Ignore the chorus,
Or hate in the crowds,
Keep looking up,
Hate,
Love,
Maybe fate,
If love is there,
Your life will be fair,
Keep looking up.

Skye Berwick (12)
Conisborough College, Catford

To The Teachers Of 2021

To the teachers of 2021
You helped us face the hard times of Covid-19
You helped us face the hard times of wearing face masks
You helped us get good marks on our tests

To the teachers of 2021
You made education fun and funny
You made our school a better place and safe
You made education easy to learn

To the teachers of 2021
You helped us hold the ropes tight
You helped us be better people
You helped us plan a better life for ourselves

To the teachers of 2021
You helped us be stronger
You helped us face challenges in life
You helped us without making a face

To the teachers of 2021
You taught us well even when we fell
You helped us at the worst times
You gave us the opportunity to succeed

Thank you for facing the hard times with us.

Trevell Pinnock (12)
Conisborough College, Catford

Unexpected

I would not expect
You to talk to me
You're the person that's social
A person that is accepted by everyone
But yet you talk to me

I would not expect
To know who you truly are
How happy but sad
How social but alone
You are the opposite of what I thought and show

I would not expect
Me to think that tomorrow you're not there
Me to think that tomorrow is our last
And that tomorrow is the end
The end of everything

I would expect
Me not to forget
Me not to forgive
Me to accept that it is the end
The end of the years, months, days I spent
For nothing but I still remember.
And that is the unexpected.

Goda Liorancaite (13)
Conisborough College, Catford

Growing Up

Growing up would be fun they said
But it goes by quick
For as long as I could remember
I wanted to be older
When I was eight
I wanted to be ten
When I was ten
I wanted to be fifteen

Now I don't want to grow up
Growing up is growing old
It's like getting closer to death every day
Getting a job
Having a family
Raising a family
Owning a house
By growing up
And by growing old
I need all of these things

Growing up is
Forcing yourself to be happy
Growing up is
Mandatory

I understand everyone has to grow up eventually
And I wish I didn't grow up so soon
I'm still young
Even though the days feel long
The years are short.

Ellie Dorey (13)
Conisborough College, Catford

We Need To Act Fast

When does our planet ever get tranquillity?

Ice caps seek revenge by collapsing as expeditiously as a flicker of the human eye
Sea levels are rising and engulfing our land
Tsunamis are crashing harder than ever before, taking their indignation out on everyone
Floods are swallowing the exposed ecosystems
Tornadoes are whizzing, revealing the nature of the world
Hurricanes are concealing the potential dangers
Droughts are dominating districts, caging people in like zoo animals

We don't have enough time left...
We need to take action now...
We must start invigorating our world...
Before it becomes inevitable...
Before it turns into a massacre...

Dilvesh Gopinath (15)
Conisborough College, Catford

Rise Like A Phoenix

Darkness while sitting in the corner
Nobody listens and nobody helps
All they say is "Ignore them"
Then they walk away as if it was always that simple
The laughing echoes in my brain
My mind is filled and I'm shivering with pain
I mean it is in my brain
It's in my veins
But nothing will change
The fact that they shattered me into pieces
But in the end, I lose hope
But I need to rise up
Pick up the pieces
Leave them behind
Because I'm going to rise up
Pick up the pieces and leave them behind
Because I'm going to rise up like a phoenix against you
I'm not a toy for you to mess with so I rise.

Sanaa Safi (12)
Conisborough College, Catford

Dreams Come True

Dreams are in our sleep
When we dream we see stuff
But this is what I see in my dreams
I see myself in the year 2027 graduating
I see myself going to a prestigious school
I see myself finishing school
I see myself doing my dream job
Being a doctor
I see that I have everything done
I have got into the school I wanted
I have become the doctor I wanted to be
Dreams can come true
Just believe in yourself
You just need to believe harder in yourself
When you wake up you might be upset that it is just a dream
But if you believe in yourself you will achieve everything you want to achieve
Because dreams do and will come true one day.

Fahima Daum (11)
Conisborough College, Catford

Future Self

Dear future self,
One of the few things I ask,
Always speak up,
Don't let the light shine through you.

Dear future self,
One of the few things I ask,
Don't let people stamp all over you,
Because eventually you will feel worthless.

Dear future self,
One of the few things I ask,
Remember not to fake a smile,
Even if your true self shows.

Dear future self,
One of a few things I ask,
Let out your feelings to the people around you,
Pick up your phone and ring someone.

Dear future self,
One of a few things I ask,
Don't give up,
Follow your dreams.

Ruby-Rae Parsons (13)
Conisborough College, Catford

True Love

True love is a miracle, it really is.
Her skin glows in the glimmering sun
My eyes reflect the glistening moonlight
I'm covered in the colours of you
We stay strong together through and through
Some days I repeat over and over:
Why am I like this?
Love is love is it not?
So why are slurs and insulting words hurled my way every day?
But there's a hole that you fill
You're as lovely as a summer's day
And I still don't know how you came to be mine.
People still hate us today as we lay
But in my mind you continue to shine
And we loved ourselves anyway.

Blessing Osahon (13)
Conisborough College, Catford

It's Not Just You!

It's not just you, we all feel blue,
And yes, it's true.
Do you know what people go through?
I can tell you feel down
So don't be scared to frown.
It's okay to just ignore it as your young self is hoping for a crown.
My life isn't going well
But I don't fall,
I stand tall.
It's okay to show a tear,
Why fear?
Yes life is full of ups and downs,
That's why we see so many frowns.
It's okay, as long as you try,
Just try and stand as tall as the sky.
Just don't let your young self down
And leave him with a frown.

Joshua Harding (12)
Conisborough College, Catford

Dreams

Dreams can run as long as it takes to catch up
It depends on how you focus on yourself
It depends on how I focus on me
My dream is to be a footballer
Ever since I was three
I'm not giving up for the world
Because I'm planning to succeed
I'm not going to listen to the bad, only to the good
Because if I get knocked down seven times
I will get back up on the eighth
Dreams keep you up at night
Even at the darkest of times
But at the moment you are satisfied with the results
Even after a night of silent cries
To all the haters...
I will try!

Cairo Faria (12)
Conisborough College, Catford

I Wish...

I wish that
In the future everyone
Will be happy and
There will be
No violence.

I wish that
In the future I
Will become an amazing
Audiologist and help people.

I wish that
In the future my
Mum will be alive and
Help me when I need her.

I wish that
In the future I
Will get my driving license
Early and get a job with a good pay cheque
So I can help my family and friends.

I wish that
In my future my friend
Will be successful and have an amazing life
Like a lion winning a race.

Husna Shahin (13)
Conisborough College, Catford

Religion And Lies

R eligion, religion, religion,
E veryone's questions are the same,
L ike once is not enough!
I nside, I'm bursting but I can't say anything,
G oing on, I know my religion is very special,
I know they just want to embarrass themselves,
O n top of that, you're speaking behind my back,
N o, nothing will make me feel misrepresented.

L ies, lies, lies,
I n your mind, you know you're guilty,
E xcept, you won't tell the truth,
S top, enough is enough!

Alishba Zara Malik (12)
Conisborough College, Catford

Sometimes

Sometimes I know it is difficult to believe in you
When people say no
Sometimes I know it is difficult to defend yourself
When there is no one around you
Sometimes I know it is difficult when you are hopeless and see life go by
Sometimes I know you see life like a big challenge
As a big mountain to climb
I know you are young but you are still strong
Sometimes I know the beginning is not perfect as wish
But it is time to change your mind the way you see life
It is time for you to prove and be proud of yourself
Repeat: 'I know who I am'.

N'guessan Naomie (13)
Conisborough College, Catford

Careless

We say equal rights; you say equal fights,
We say equality; you say misogyny,
We say it's racism; you say it's just a word,
If it doesn't exist why are we still being oppressed?
You say we're equal but we are still being told how to dress,
If your dress is 'too short' you're a w****,
If your dress is too long, you're a prude and no one will want you!
If you're skinny you need to eat more,
If you're bigger you need to take a rest, regain your figure,
We're screaming for help but you couldn't care less!

Naomi Okojie (14)
Conisborough College, Catford

Your Decision, Your Life

My life, my choice,
My choice, my future,
My future, my destiny,
Choose how and where you take your life,
One wrong decision could take your life down the wrong path,
One could be the greatest at what they do,
But once they pick up a knife and ruin their whole life,
There are three possible endings:
They could end up dead, in prison or on the run,
But in the process of ending someone's life,
They're ruining their own life,
Always remember there are consequences for everything,
Your decision, your life.

Tobi Adebayo (14)
Conisborough College, Catford

Future Me

In the future I would like to keep humble
In the future I don't want any drama
In the future I want a good reputation
In the future I want a good life

In the future I want to stay happy
In the future there will be ups and downs
But hopefully it will come back around
In the future I will have a good career
In the future I want a good life

In the future I will be persistent
In the future I will have a nice house
In the future I will have a great family
In the future I want a good life.

Savanna Seck (11)
Conisborough College, Catford

Some People

Some things you see online are not real
They use filters, make-up and have wounds that won't heal
Some people can't even keep down a meal
Some people think you don't care how they feel
Some people are less able than others
And not everyone has fathers and mothers
Some people don't have a place to live
But all we can do is be there for each other
You are who you are meant to be
Stay who you are and be free
If you're worried you will soon see
You're empowered.

Abby Stevens (13)
Conisborough College, Catford

Person In Power

In this world, it seems as if the only voices heard are those in power
To be in power, is to withhold a status in society
Where your decision determines the future of ours

But to be honest
We all have power in which we control
It makes no difference
If it's by nature or not
To make a change by using our resources
Should be our goal

Even if it feels like you aren't being heard
You should still make a sound...
No matter how little change will be found.

Shayanne Barrie (14)
Conisborough College, Catford

Save The World

Plastic in the oceans
Plastic in nature
Please save our planet
The pollution in the air
Trees being cut into shreds
Just for paper to be used once
Please save our planet
CO2 being released as quickly as quick as a virus
Destroying the ozone layer
Please save our world
Just stop what you are doing and listen
Listen to your daughter
Listen to your grandson
Is this right for them?
Do you want them to live in a future world of pain and regret?
Do you...?

Molly O'Dwyer (12)
Conisborough College, Catford

To My Dreams

Dreams in my brain
Sleep with my eyes closed
Things going through my head
Bad and good people are in dreams
Imagination...
People, real people, all different people

Dreams in my brain
Good and bad things happen in dreams
Violence, future, unexpected situations
All these could happen in everyone's dream
Before you know it you will have your GCSE papers right in front of you
Time goes by so fast when you are dreaming
It feels like you have time travelled.

Giruththikan Navinathan (12)
Conisborough College, Catford

What's Your Dream?

Devastatingly damaging dreams
Ambitious dreams or unimaginable, unthinkable dreams
What do you dream of?
Months go by and what do you remember?
June, July, August and September
Life doesn't go on forever
And now you already surrender
Life is a chance
Life is valuable
Life is a mission since once it is over
It's over
Your dreams don't lie by you
Do you really need a clue?
You already thought it through
So now it's time to be true.

Arvin Ramnarace (12)
Conisborough College, Catford

We Are Not The Same

We are not the same,
Some people are black,
Some people are white,
And some people are brown,
So we shouldn't discriminate.
Some people have problems,
And some people are disabled,
But that doesn't matter.
We are like apples or potatoes,
We all have different colours,
Different shapes,
The seeds aren't all exactly in the same spot,
So we should never discriminate.
Some people have different personalities,
And different families.

Jacob Byckovas (11)
Conisborough College, Catford

I'm Not Okay

My mask is slowly cracking
Every time I smile a crack appears
Every time I laugh at someone's jokes a crack appears
I say I'm okay when I'm not okay
I say I'm fine when I'm not
I look in the mirror and smile at myself
My reflection always frowns at me
I can't handle my reflection
Look at my reflection
See if it smiles
See if it laughs
See if it's the person I always wanted to be
Then I soon realised that I was loved.

Eseasa Bracewell (11)
Conisborough College, Catford

Age Doesn't Matter

Age doesn't matter,
Kids can give a tip,
Old people are gold,
It doesn't matter how old you are,
Kids can be smart,
The elderly can be strong,
Don't discriminate by age,
Children should have rights,
Adults should be able to have fun,
It shouldn't just be kids having fun,
Children should be able to vote,
No such thing as 'you're too young',
There is no such thing as 'too old',
Age doesn't matter.

Kabiian Linkeswaran (12)
Conisborough College, Catford

My Future Dreams

My future dreams,
To build a team,
And plant a tree,
To help the environment grow.

My future dreams,
All we need,
Is some hope and positivity,
To let the world walk beside us.

My future dreams,
Let us all come together,
To build a better future,
For our children's generation.

So I'll say it again,
If you care about the children,
Let us come together,
To give us a better future.

Luke Rafferty (12)
Conisborough College, Catford

Racism

Racist slurs are not welcome on Earth
Racism is the worst thing on Earth
Stop racism from being a problem we face
Racism is something we need to think about
It doesn't matter if someone is a different race
It's all about the Earth God made
Stop racism from being a problem we face
God wants us to live in peace
Stop being racist!
Make Earth feel like an oasis
Please listen to this poem and make Earth a better place.

Raaqul Senthuran (12)
Conisborough College, Catford

My Name...

My name is Rose,
I know my identity is a mystery.
I like to play games and sing,
And dance and daydream.
I don't like school that much,
And I do karate.
I am completely random,
I know I'm weird,
I might ask myself things.

Yeah, everyone is different,
In their very own way,
People might think differently of me,
But that's fine,
Because I am happy to be myself,
And so should you.

Alisa Ram (12)
Conisborough College, Catford

Identity

We are born
We are here
We are alive
But why?
We live in this society
We live in this world full of hierarchy and power
People come from nothing to something
Or something to nothing
We live in a world where smart people thrive
Yet dumb thrive
Anything to get alive
Illegal or legal
It really doesn't matter...
They are they, you are you
Them are them
But then
Who are you?

Iyanu Stephens (13)
Conisborough College, Catford

To Myself

To my dear future me
I will change the society
How people treat each other

To my dear future me
Believe in yourself and keep moving forward

To my dear future me
I want you to be a symbol of peace to the next generation

To my dear future me
It's better to hold a poor hand
Than a rich hand

To my dear future me
Focus on yourself
Then focus on other people.

Murtaza Wakili (13)
Conisborough College, Catford

World

World,
The greatest word,
People dying but people also forget that the world is yet to die.

World,
Earth is going,
Humans are dying because of the war that they did not want to be in,
Animals are becoming extinct because we take them for granted.

World
I know you're leaving,
But everyone keeps forgetting,
I love you and I am glad to know you,
'Cause you are my world.

Chantelle Lubega Naiga (12)
Conisborough College, Catford

Our World

These days body image is different to so many people
Why do girls have to look a certain way?
If you're skinny, you have an eating disorder
If you seem overweight, you need to eat less
If you dress nicely, you want attention
But if you don't overdress, you don't care about yourself
See, no matter what you do, people will always judge
This is why you should do what makes you happy and
makes you.

Samantha Vera Vargas (11)
Conisborough College, Catford

Try

I can't do this
I try
I always try so hard but it is never enough for me
For my friends, for my family
I try so hard to make them proud
To help them when they need it
But I always seem to fail
I try to help myself with my future
With my career but I just seem to always push myself down
I want to try harder but it's too hard to try
I'm trying...
But trying is never enough.

Nicole Stocki (13)
Conisborough College, Catford

Future Me!

Dear future me,
I'll ask you one thing,
Will I have a passionate boyfriend?
Will I have a business or a job?
Will I have kids? A boy or a girl?

Dear future me,
I'll have the best car in the world,
But be mixed with a swirl,
I'd be happy as a rainbow,
But I'd be sad as a halo.

Dear future me,
Will I be kind and help my family?
Huh? Dear future me!

Kainat Sahrai (12)
Conisborough College, Catford

Dear Past Me

Dear past me,
I have only one thing to tell you,
Believe in your dreams,
Trust me, one day, you'll feel your dream,
Dear past me,
Don't listen to the people that tell you you can't do it,
Because you'll do it,
Don't be shy,
'Cause you'll shine,
You'll fly,
And remember, you're a star.
One day, you'll achieve your goals,
So give it a go.

Paul Manhan Yoro (12)
Conisborough College, Catford

Memories Of The Loss

Every loss
Every memory
You held my hand
Through thick and thin
Made me realise where I've been
Now you're gone
How can I hold on?
We made a promise when I was young

It's been the hardest year now
Memories of a life that's been loved
Flying free in the deep night sky
Sparkling down to life
Every dream we grip on to
Gives us life to hold and love.

Paige Lewis-Fleming (12)
Conisborough College, Catford

Don't Give Up

Dear future self,
Don't give up!
Don't be a scaredy-cat,
Don't be afraid to stand up for yourself,
Don't give up,
I am not afraid of anything,
But I hope you aren't too.
Don't give up!
There will be lots of danger,
Don't give up,
Because eventually,
It's going to go away anyway,
Anything that is stopping you,
Will always go away, always.

Jasitha Chanthiraseelan (12)
Conisborough College, Catford

Difference Is Beauty

E veryone is different
M others have unique children
P eople are never the same
O thers may think they are sane
W e may all change
E ven then we will never be the same
R estricting your personality won't change you
E mpower yourself and be free
D oing that will make you happy

M y life is happy
E mpower me.

Harun Abubakar (11)
Conisborough College, Catford

Onika Supreme

This time
This monument
This era
A rap legend was higher than ever
Where she reigned both and sea
And has many sons you see
Her rhymes and flows inspire those who want some more
A queen of rap
Supreme and empowers
Those who want to dream
To dream beyond the stars and sea
And enter a land where dreams come true
And inspire a generation
That hard work is really true.

Gladys Awok (14)
Conisborough College, Catford

Normality

What is normal?
Black, brown, white, purple, pink, blue,
Is there a normal?
What is normal?
'Terrorist', 'bomber',
'I forgot you have to stay sober',
What does that mean?
Normality is like a facility of different places, races, hair colour, eye colour.
What does normal mean?
Do you have to look a certain way to fit into a certain place?
What is normal?

Aaliya Kachwala (11)
Conisborough College, Catford

Let Your Opinion Be Free

Don't encage it
Don't put chains on it
Let it be free

Let it fly
Let it try
Let it be free

Your opinion is your choice
Don't let others pull it back
Let others be informed by it
Don't let them stab it in the back

Don't keep it to yourself
Let others hear it
Protest and encourage it
Don't let others tear it.

April Hoang (12)
Conisborough College, Catford

Believe

B e ambitious, be who you want to be
E scape from the things that make you weak
L ove what you do and what's right for you
I f you want to be happy then you'll find this is true
E verything that makes you feel free
V isualise and it'll come to be
E ffort and time is all you need and your dreams are sure to come true eventually.

Ryan Johnson (12)
Conisborough College, Catford

Future Me

Dear future me
I wanna be something important
Follow your dream and never look back
Fly high as you possibly can and reach the stars

Dear future me
I wanna tell you all but just ghost and vanish
Don't listen people
Work hard
Make money last for longer

Dear future me
Remember to keep focussed
And help others
Keep family and friends.

Gianluca Vargas (13)
Conisborough College, Catford

I Want, I Hope

When I'm older I want hope for a lot of stuff
When I'm older I want to be successful
When I'm older I hope to be a better person
When I'm older I want to be healthy
When I'm older I hope to be good
When I'm older I want a house
When I'm older I want some pets
When I'm older I want to be organised
When I'm older I want to be a vet.

Rachel Katkovska (12)
Conisborough College, Catford

Dreams

I won't give up until the day I die
I'm not going to die until my dream comes true
They said, "You are just throwing it all away just for one stupid dream
Dreams don't come true and you're dead!"
I am not going to die until I have accomplished my dream
I am stronger and better
You won't win either way
Because I am not giving up!

Faiz Haroon (11)
Conisborough College, Catford

Being Judged

You will always be judged
About your skin
About your religion
Also about your culture

You can be judged about the littlest of things
About your nails
About your style
Even about your body

These things can put you down
They can degrade your personality
Bring down who you are
So don't let nasty comments get to you.

Priya-Sherone Blackwood (12)
Conisborough College, Catford

Family

Family is my world
Family is the most important thing in my life
I love my parents and everyone who is related to me
I take care and look after them at all times
They will always be with me
They empower me all the time
All I care about is my family
We always bake, clean and watch movies together
I love my family
Family is everything.

Antonia Calinchin (12)
Conisborough College, Catford

I Have A Dream

I have a dream
That there is peace in the world
And that there will be no more
Wars and only eternal peace

I have a dream
To inspire people to be the best
They can and to become
A very good person in life

I have a dream
To support all charities
Always follow the path of God
To show me the way of pure life.

Jamie Paiva (13)
Conisborough College, Catford

Me...

I never caused harm,
All of these insults because of my skinny arms,
Why me?

Why have I been bullied since 13?
Why can't I be like the others?
Always criticising me and my brothers!

I always focus in class,
Receiving threats,
Expecting me not to grass,
I have no friends,
Almost like walking into dead ends.

Ryan Smith (13)
Conisborough College, Catford

Retro Gaming

Gaming. What would I do without it?
Gaming. It inspires me
Gaming. It tires me
Gaming. It's crazy
It keeps me happy
So many games
It kind of scares me really
TBH, where do I start?
A Nintendo Switch or the PSS?
Both have a high resolution, screen and graphics
But in terms of raw hard-drive power
The PSS takes it!

Daniel Kouma (12)
Conisborough College, Catford

Climate Change

The world is warmer,
More pollution,
The world right now,
Is in a bad position.

Deforestation is happening,
And it is baffling,
The world is crumbling,
While we are mumbling.

The world will be better,
If we do all we can to stop all of this,
It will be a safer place,
And will have better traits.

Oliver Scott (12)
Conisborough College, Catford

It's All Down To You

It's all down to you to make a change
It's all down to you to make a difference
Something inside of me makes me believe in you
So I know what I can do
If so, let's see you make that change
That difference
You go and pass this message on to someone else
Trust me, you can empower someone
Like I empowered you.

Lucy Martine Bennett (12)
Conisborough College, Catford

My Ambitions

Like a boy that wishes a lot
Of things happening
My hopes are to get better at sports
Especially athletics and football
They are my favourite

My dreams
I am always thinking about becoming a streamer
That is a YouTuber
Dreams, hopes, ambitions
They will always be my passions and supported.

Ibrahim El Deyasti (11)
Conisborough College, Catford

Dear Future Me

Dear future me,
One thing I want to ask you is,
How are you and how is your life going?

Dear future me,
Do you have a business?
Where are you working?

Dear future me,
Am I happy with life?

Dear future me,
How is my relationship with my family?
Bye, future me.

Zolai Shor (11)
Conisborough College, Catford

I Don't Care

Your words don't hurt me,
I'm stronger than your comments,
You preach your lies,
I don't care,
I'm bigger, stronger, saner,
Than you,
Call me 'fat', call me 'ugly',
I'm stronger than your words,
I know I'm perfect in my own way,
I am me.

Taylor Robinson (12)
Conisborough College, Catford

Hey Future Self

Hey future self,
I ask you one thing,
To show the path that you bring,
All the questions gather up in my head,
Cannot even help myself when I'm in bed,
I want to ask you what job I will get,
And also make sure I will not regret,
And leave this world before the end.

Alia Daum (11)
Conisborough College, Catford

You Are...

Y ou're amazing in every way
O bviously, you have a say
U nderstanding you is easy

A nd your jokes are kind of cheesy
R esilient not a coward
E ven if you don't feel it...

You are empowered!

Tia Lye-Corne (13)
Conisborough College, Catford

Hey You!

Hey you, over there
With the pretty long hair
Don't be afraid
Put your hair in a braid
Don't care what people think

Be proud of yourself
Look how far you have come
Don't give up now
It's too late for that!

Dejuntee Dogley (13)
Conisborough College, Catford

Ivory Coast

Ivory Coast, the place I call home
With calm distant singing
And the sizzling of oil cooking
Ivory Coast, the place I call home
With rowing boats
And the laughing of kids enjoying life
Ivory Coast, the place I call home.

Eliora Eyou-Mel (12)
Conisborough College, Catford

Identity

Identity is you,
Identity is what you stand for,
Identity makes you, you,
Identity is who you are,
Identity is us,
Us as a community,
Identity is often defined by us,
Identity is a mystery.

Hayley Conlon (12)
Conisborough College, Catford

What You Are

What you are is unique
What you are is amazing
What you are is good
And what you are is the person reading this poem
And the writer of this poem, Ibrahim
Would like you to know that you are awesome!

Ibrahim Turvey (12)
Conisborough College, Catford

My Future And My Present

To future me
Take all the opportunities coming your way
Don't let anyone stop you
Focus on school, you could be something
Be the best version of you
Work your hardest!

Khloe Michael (12)
Conisborough College, Catford

To My Future Self

To my future self
It's the 12th of May 2022, I am fourteen
I'm nearly in Year 10 but not quite yet
I wonder what my future will be like
Or if I will achieve my dreams
Sometimes I doubt myself
But I know I can rely on myself

Because I work hard every day
I try my best in class
I love my friends and they love me
I can't wait for Year 10
But I am afraid
I am afraid that I will mess up
Or that I will stop trying my best
Or that I will lose my friends
I'm afraid I will mess up my school work
Or that I will fail my tests
But at the end of the day
I know that I can rely on myself

Because I work hard every day
I try my best in class
I love my friends and they love me
I can't wait for Year 10

And to my future self
If you are afraid
As long as you try your best
And cherish your friends
You can rely on yourself too.

Oliver Thompson (14)
Dyke House Academy, Hartlepool

Standards

I get so angry
I must be 'on my period'
He gets mad
He needs some 'space'

I love female singers
I'm such a 'girl'
He loves female singers
He's a feminist

I speak up about politics
I don't know what I'm talking about
He speaks about politics
Everyone listens

I wear a tank top
I'm showing 'too much'
He wears a tank top
It's a warm day

I'm a stay-at-home mother
It's expected of me
He is a stay-at-home dad
He is breaking the gender norms and trying his best

I have a lot of exes
I'm a s***
He has lots of exes
He's a player

'I'm so sick of running as fast as I can
Wondering if I'd get there quicker as a man!'

Isabelle Kay (14)
Dyke House Academy, Hartlepool

My Inspiring Planet

Our Earth has seen the best and worst of times
All of the species that inhabit here
Our Earth has been through all of our sublimes
We need equality and that is clear

The Suffragettes are women I would thank
This small movement went down in history
And Rosa Parks is high up on my rank
Many people were contradictory

I'm feminist but men have played their part
MLK Junior had preached his dreams
Both men's and women's ways have been quite smart
Kept going when things were not as they seemed
Inspiring people, who we could all be
Since we're here now, change the world, let's be free!

Sarah Arnett (14)
Dyke House Academy, Hartlepool

What Makes Me... Me?

What makes me... me?
Is it how I look or how I lead?
Being me helps me to succeed.
This opportunity lets you know all about my identity.
Now let me begin,
What makes me... me?
Pursuing my visions and my dreams.
It's hard to ask, I'm only 14.
Do I travel the world or help those in need?
It can be strange to wonder,
This is our society.
Yet I still ask myself, what makes me... me?
I want to take action,
Make others feel free -
Educate the world for all eternity.
I am filled with compassion -
From my head to my toes.
I just want to show.
What makes me... me after all?

Emily Kimmel (14)
Dyke House Academy, Hartlepool

Daydreaming

Sometimes I will lie on my bed
And dream some lovely dreams
Like sitting on a rock
Watching a beautiful stream

Sometimes I will lie on my bed
And dream some impossible dreams
Like growing massive eagle wings
And flying towards the sun's gleam

Sometimes I will lie on my bed
And dream some crazy dreams
Like designing vehicles with a dragon
Making things like tanks with laser beams

Sometimes I will lie on my bed
And dream some breathtaking dreams
Like climbing up a mountain
And being a part of an exploration team.

Connie Robertson (12)
Dyke House Academy, Hartlepool

The Willow Tree

I have always liked to wonder
What is below down under
I live in a village with a crystal palace
Down under filled with malice is all there is to see

Dinner time is almost here
And its malice is getting near
Its power is like a rose
Dropping wherever it goes
Lots of lives have been lost
All for what cost?

I hear the dinner bells chiming
And all I can do is keep rhyming
All I want is for the willlow tree to fade
Just like the food on my plate
Unfortunately we share and go
Will I survive?
I hope so!

Shay Mulcahy (11)
Dyke House Academy, Hartlepool

Food

Food's the best
It helps me rest
When I'm in the nest
People are in poverty
Why don't you see?
They need food
So empower me

Turkey or chicken
It's all finger-licking
But why won't you listen?
People need food
To help with their mood
If you don't I'll have you sued

So help us out
I won't scream and shout
Or dance about
Just help those in need
Let them be freed
And plant the seed
And empower thee.

Charley Stuart (14)
Dyke House Academy, Hartlepool

Get Lost In A Book

Snuggle up
Grab a book
Turn the crisp white pages
Enter into a world of wonders
Getting lost in the ages
Endless amounts of empowering tales
Unlock imagination with curiosity to inhale
From the Vikings to Rome
All whilst at home
Retreat in whatever book you prefer
Science and stories, a dragon in a lair
A world full of authors to explore
From J K Rowling to Applebaum, you'll certainly want more
So whilst in your cosy snook
Get lost in your favourite book.

Freya Light (11)
Dyke House Academy, Hartlepool

The Opposite Gender

I'm happy being me
But sometimes I wonder
What it would be like
As the opposite gender
Some days I can't even look at myself in the mirror
Knowing what I am isn't what I want to be
So I wish I were a boy
So I don't have to deal with the hatred that my body brings
But if I want a chance
Medically is the only way
Otherwise others may say
"But you're a girl, stop pretending!"
It's not fair
Why did I have to be born in the wrong body?

Sophie Hall (12)
Dyke House Academy, Hartlepool

Women

"You should smile more," he said as he looked me up and down smirking
"Have you gained weight?" he said as they all laughed
"You look so tired," he said as he pushed me into his friends
"You look rubbish without make-up," he said as he looked at me in disgust
"What was she wearing?"
"Go make me a sandwich!"
We are women
How dare we not be perfect!
We are women
How dare we dress the way we want!
How dare we be us!

Sena Durmus (13)
Dyke House Academy, Hartlepool

This Is Good Education

Education is good for your brain
In fact I go to school on a train
My name is Lexie and I like to play basketball and we play it in the hall
I love my teacher
Especially Miss Keith the PE teacher
When she shows us how to do something
I'm in belief
Whatever she does, she says well done
But her PE lessons are so fun
Also I love maths because I'm good
When I get home I have a friendly neighbourhood
It feels like I am a part of the family.

Lexie Greig (11)
Dyke House Academy, Hartlepool

The Colony

Some ants look for food
To feed their own colony
They put in the effort
But it's for 'we' and not 'me'

Some ants dig tunnels
More room for the colony
They did it for their friends
But not for themselves
Well, maybe

The queen lays eggs
New ants for the colony
She's the mother of all, the pinnacle of royalty

But us humans, what could we be?
Because this doesn't feel like a colony.

Hayden Mason (14)
Dyke House Academy, Hartlepool

Justice For Ukraine

It all started with Putin wanting his people home
But the Ukraine cities wanted to be alone
They took a part of Crimea
But we didn't want them near
So we stood up here
And made them flee with fear

They then wanted a bombardment late at night
But we let them know we would stay and fight

The bombs crashed down upon the land
Left huge craters in the sand
Bombs flew over heads
Millions of innocent citizens found dead.

Hayden Menzies (13)
Dyke House Academy, Hartlepool

Rainbow Flag

A flag waves up high
Its vibrant stripes glitter and swirl
As graceful as a bird, it swoops and turns
It's a symbol
Of love and pride
For him, her, them
No matter how many times it's torn down
Though stone walls tower
We fight for them to fall
In their place we raise our flag
Its rainbow shining through the darkness
And as it flutters through shine and storm
We'll never forget those who struggled for it all.

Molly Davison (15)
Dyke House Academy, Hartlepool

If I Were Magic

If I were magic
The people would be equal
Heritage, race, creed, gender, sexuality
None of these things would matter
If I were magic
There would be no war
There would be no hate
If I were magic
There would only be love
There would be love for each and every person
There would be love for each and every animal
There would be love for the Earth
And there would be love for cultures
If I were magic.

Alfie Lodge (14)
Dyke House Academy, Hartlepool

Bullies

Trapped in a cave by their voices
I'm always questioning their choices
It seems all I do is cry in my room
I hope that a silent night will come soon
These monsters just won't leave
Even when I plead and plead
Why won't they leave me alone?
Even when I am in my zone
The bullying continues on my phone
It feels like there is no end in sight
I am tired of this fight
To all of you, I say goodnight.

Emma Newton (13)
Dyke House Academy, Hartlepool

Our Mother Needs You

Deep in the woods they lie
Starving and crying
With hope of living
With hope of someone saving them

But who?
Who can help the species
The endangered species
Who?

We can
But are you friendly
To your mother
To your mother of nature?

We need you
Your mother needs you
To save the environment
So join the journey
Of our mother nature?

Danushan Rajasekaram (13)
Dyke House Academy, Hartlepool

I'm A Soccer Lover

To play on the field
Until my player is healed
My friends, my coaches and me
Wide-open space to run free

Do some tricks
Round the players
Here we go
Let your passion show

Shoot some goals, one by one
What's that? You're having fun

She shoots, she scored, you just won
Your season, your fans scream, let's go team!

Lakisha Allenden (15)
Dyke House Academy, Hartlepool

Make A Change

If we do not make a change
Birds will no longer fly
The Earth will eventually die
If we make a change
People will not die
The Earth will keep alive
Ice caps will not melt
If we clear the danger
We have felt change today
All fears will fade away
At the end of the day
Everyone will be better off
If we make a change today.

Jay Wintersgill (13)
Dyke House Academy, Hartlepool

The Importance Of Education

In the future, education helps
No one knows how it helps
But it does
It helps you get a job
People who failed school and stopped education growing up
They will tell you how they lost all their things
Use your education wisely
Get an amazing future for yourself
It will always improve your life and your intelligence.

Darcie Belben (12)
Dyke House Academy, Hartlepool

Rugby World

Rugby links people
And empowers their views
And gives people opportunities
To go on the local news

Doesn't matter if you are small or tall
Strong or weak
All that matters is you have the determination to peak

The atmosphere is loud
A chance for people to meet
Also to watch great rugby.

Sonny Wintersgill (14)
Dyke House Academy, Hartlepool

Change

Maybe they are uneducated
Or maybe the education system failed them all
Maybe it's because they're women
But I think they deserve more
Change, it is promised
Yet it is scarce
The ones who birth your children
The ones who do it all
Treated like nothing
Nothing at all.

Ellie Emmerson (14)
Dyke House Academy, Hartlepool

Nature

Roses are as soft as silk
Daisies are as white as milk
Snowballs are elegant like the rich
Tulips leaning towards the deep, dark ditch
Trucks and lorries come here for money
Even though it means stealing a bee's honey
You're stealing our home and everything we know!

Georgia Roberts
Dyke House Academy, Hartlepool

Sleep

I am not an interesting person
I have no radical views on the world
I like to eat
I like to sleep
And that is okay
My bed is my favourite place
When life is stressful I eat cake
I am a simple person
And that is okay
I'd rather sleep than stay awake.

Matilda Kier (13)
Dyke House Academy, Hartlepool

Money

I love money
Spending is funny
Retail therapy
Makes me happy

I buy candles
They smell nice
People buy sandals
Then wear them twice

I'm always shopping online
Making things mine.

Hollie Willingham (14)
Dyke House Academy, Hartlepool

Power

They ridicule us
They pull our hair and cuss
Too curly, too nappy, too straight or in braids
Most times we are not who people want to date
Even if we are of the same complexion
They will blame it on a 'ghetto' impression
And when they provoke us, we are suddenly loud
And then silenced from making another sound
They will tear black women into a single piece
And then wonder why our emotions increase
If we are pretty or a big, they think we are ugly
Comparing us to other black women doesn't make us feel bubbly
Our hair, our lips and our styles are all pros
And we will not apologise for our 'fros
We will blossom like a beautiful flower
Because what I know about black women is that we have power...

Jadesola Odukoya (16)
Hendon School, Hendon

You Can...

Day can turn into night,
Night can turn into day,
That's the way it goes,
People come and go,
They say hi and bye,
Every day is the same,
Some people leave you,
Some betray,
And you wish they would just go away,
There is no such thing as friends,
They are just there to give you the support that you think you need
Of course they are important,
To make you feel more confident,
But sometimes they are the people that let you down the most,
But they don't mean anything,
And I know it's heartbreaking,
But it's their loss,
You're worth much more than that.
So don't do it,
Don't take a rope or a knife and end your life,
We all need you,
God put you here on this world for a reason,
And in this situation, you will have to figure it out by yourself,

Life is short, don't waste it thinking you are a failure,
Don't put yourself under pressure
And endless torture.
There's a doctor
To help.
So take control
And I'm not saying you don't need anyone,
I'm saying that you have more power than you think
And it's your choice to use them or not.

Amina Amoyeva (13)
Hendon School, Hendon

2022

It's 2022 and the world is ending
More animals are extinct and they're descending
And not to mention we need more trees
Can somebody help us please

Factories are working every day
While there are large fires far away
Sea levels rising
While animals are dying

While we are out spending money
Fish in the ocean are dying lonely
Let's work as a team
Easy we will make it seem.

Rayanne Moussa (11)
Hendon School, Hendon

You Can Stop This

Ice caps are melting
Animals are dying
You can stop this
By recycling plastic

The Earth isn't just a floating ball
It's a planet about to get destroyed
You can stop this
By picking up litter

Why don't you do your part?
It will help
Not much but it's a start
So if we all come together
We can stop it
Once and for all.

Karim Bassioni (11)
Hendon School, Hendon

You Are You

Why should we care what other people think?
Why do their opinions always make us rethink
What if we thought that we are perfect as we are?
I don't know why we don't think that it is just bizarre
Take the critical voice and throw it in the bin
If we did that we would be on a win
Whether that's a voice in your head or people in the world
It should be ignored and ripped away, hurled
We should love the skin we are given
You are you, individual, different, you don't need to be forgiven
You are you, treat yourself with respect
Then you will see a whole different prospect
You are you, remember these words whenever you are down
You are you, you should never ever frown.

Lillie Harris (13)
Huntercombe Hospital School, Taplow

My Home

My body is my home but I feel this house isn't right for me
The windows are shattered
The curtains have holes
And the front door's all broken and battered

My body is my home yet I feel trapped in a stranger's abode
The furniture is weird and uncomfy
The scent isn't just quite right
The channels aren't the same on the telly
And the shower head's not at the right height

My body is my home yet it's not perfect
My bedroom walls aren't the right colour
I don't have my ideal settee
My bathroom sink's a bit dodgy
But I'm learning to live my life as me.

Marianne Underwood (13)
Huntercombe Hospital School, Taplow

Better Days

I am myself, not anything else
I get stares but no longer find the need to care
I'm fine with the way I am
You can't change the skin you're in
No point in trying to throw it in the bin
My scars symbolise growth and past
But could be a reminder bad things never last
All the pain and upset will dare to sneak in
But I get rid of it by dying my hair
You are you, no reason to cry in the loo
Others can judge but they have never been in your shoes
Be brave because there are always better days
Any difference you have, let it shine through
Don't worry what people think and just be you.

Keira Dunn (17)
Huntercombe Hospital School, Taplow

Eccles

Sitting in that chair
In the corner over there
With the radiators burning
Staring in the past
Being a bit cheeky and making me laugh

Shoeing horses
Making them look good
As a blacksmith always should
Driving tractors, ploughing fields
Emptying trailers of their yield

Bringing shivers back up the farm
Listening to ol' boys telling yarns
Teachers to WI
Patients to appointments

Lines and wrinkles that crease your face
Pie crust skirting around the edge
Where vibrant red had once been
Tufts of hair stick out of your ears
It hasn't grown on top for years and years

I close my eyes where I lay
Thinking about those chores I've got to do the next day.

Etholle Holt (13)
Litcham School, Litcham

All With A Touch Of A Hand

My feelings are taking over my body
Her ocean-blue eyes glisten in the sun
Her golden sandy hair bouncing around like a ball on the beach as she walks
I sit down next to her
Her soft pink lips widen and she smiles at me
I can't help myself
I reach for her hand and place it on top of hers
Her ocean-blue eyes lock with mine
My heart begins to race
Before I can say anything her soft pink lips touch mine
My mind is somewhere else
I feel her hair
It feels like clouds
My life is perfect
Who knew what the touch of a hand could do
Who knows what people think
But I do know we are something much more than friends!

Carley-Mae Sadler (13)
Litcham School, Litcham

Life, Thoughts And Emotions

Life is like roads
Lots of loads
Choices you make
Junctions you take
Every decision
Is a new vision

Thoughts are like
A bus stop you dislike
You choose where you go
Which thought waits upon
Out you go
Past the buses flow

Emotions go down
And they drown
In your head
Joy or dread
Tree of emotions
Ground full of potions
Leaves of sadness
Leaves of madness.

Lily Kayser (12)
Litcham School, Litcham

My Horse Juara

M y horse is so kind
Y ou can see how much he means to me

H e goes over jumps
O ver jumps quickly
R iding is so fun
S o I do it every day
E ven when he is angry

J uara is always angry
U p and over jumps
A ngry Juara jumps
R acing fast
A lways winning.

Leigh Penman (13)
Loudoun Academy, Galston

The Island

The...

I solated and
S tanding
L and
A lone with
N ature and surrounded by
D ocile waves

Lukas Armour (13)
Loudoun Academy, Galston

Wardrobe Of The Heart

Before I leave my house
And leave my safe cocoon
Of blankets, books and cookies
There is something I must do

Place a hat of humour on my head
So my feelings don't get hurt
A scarf of sensitivity
To remind me 'Don't be curt'

A coat of courage
Keeping me strong
Fuzzy socks of silliness
Cos my heart is still young

Mittens of modesty
To keep my ego away
A jumper of joy
So sadness won't stay

But one day, I might realise
That to myself I lied
I don't need to carry all that around
Because I have it all inside.

Sashya Nussbaum (14)
Lubavitch Senior Girls' School, London

Depression

D etached from everyone around us
E ducation, we don't have one
P ressured, trying to fit in
R ecluse, socially awkward
E scape from the world
S uppressing all our feelings
S crimmage I think it explains everything
I mpetuous, not in our vocabulary
O ver-reacting about every little thing
N ow you know how it feels to be me.

Rosa Freundlich (13)
Lubavitch Senior Girls' School, London

A Hole Inside You

What if you were shipped from joy
Or freedom down to dreams?

A pit of despair, a hole unrepaired
Inside you, going right through, right out of you

Something you can't touch, it bleeds away
You think you can't do much, thinking day after day

But don't beat yourself up, give up or stop
What will that do? It's still in you
Talk to who? No one, he won't help you
Talk to someone
He's the home run
Talk to people, to doctors, therapists and even psychologists
They know what to do, that's why they are here, to help you

What if you, to whom the hole may consume
Were given an impossible task? Thinking is your doom

Remember this, don't forget
You are you and that's what you do

It's amazing having a hole with you
But if you talk to more people
It won't hurt as much as what you think it may do.

Adam Aziri (14)
Mount St Mary's College, Spinkhill

Something

There is a start to a new
I realised that something new
Isn't always something newest
That something newest isn't always something better
We all see this someday
When the final draft or the final piece doesn't always seem better than the first sketch
But don't you enjoy it?
Finding the better version that was in the past?
Just as the dark of the dusk does come
There is a change
There is a change and to accept it and comprehend it with joy
Because the past can't and won't stop us
But don't forget it was something
The stepping stones that got us here to the present which will be
The past to the future that will come now
Enjoy yourself.

Owen He (13)
Mount St Mary's College, Spinkhill

Shut-Eyed

Their harsh words pierced me like daggers
Back to comfort I solemnly staggered

My eyes were closed
My hands were tied
My silent tears I tried to hide
A silent tear
A final wish
My depressing thoughts bad
Split apart

I departed
Success on the red carpet
With a wonderful dress

My wings burst out
So did my tears
Carried by an army of people
Who cheered.

Kaysho Stephen (12)
Mount St Mary's College, Spinkhill

Hive-Minded Media

Identity?
No, we are all bees buzzing in a hive for our queens
We need to break the chains of our captors and spread our wings
Make the one the many and the poor the rich
Destroy the media, like the hour

Media controls you
Groups you
Shows no individuality of you
A population is one shadow
While the faces are meaningless
Compare this to you
Destroy the media, live the hour.

Oliver Brown (15)
Mount St Mary's College, Spinkhill

We Are Not Alone

Are we alone
In this vast universal space?
Just one speck
Yet another race

Perhaps there is one out there
Purely made of the dark
Or another lit up
With a spark

Even more out there
Living in the sands
Possibly one more
With iron hands

So in answer
To my question
No, we aren't alone
But in fact
It is them who are on their own.

Harris King (13)
Mount St Mary's College, Spinkhill

Titanic

The ship that should sail
They said it would not fail
The singing of the whistles wail by

The voyage ventures far through the seas
Passengers pledge their life to the sea
The modern voyage vessel shall not wail by the ocean floor

There the bodies rest
Upon the ocean floor.

Natasha Reddish (11)
Mount St Mary's College, Spinkhill

Overlooked Oppression

My skin is black
My heart is not
The shock on my face
Reveals the overlooked misery
As the officer yells, "Put your hands up!"

I ache in pain
The misery insane
Injustice is very much real
And not an invention
If I'm not to be plain.

Urenna Nwamadi-Okpara (12)
Mount St Mary's College, Spinkhill

Manipulation

You betrayed me; you built me up just to take me down with you.
I was broken before, everlasting pain engraved into my skin; but you fixed me.
I believed you -
I believed you when you declared your love for me,
You never did.
You declared your obsession over me.
Love isn't demanding
Love isn't your pupils enlarging -
Passion dear whenever your gazes cross
Love is manipulation.
The twisting of words in unholy ways to strike belief -
Manipulation so good you crave it on your deathbed.
You don't lose control because of love -
You lose yourself and everything you had in the beginning.
You're useless without it.

You rely on it -
On the dark games that keep you alive when all you are is flesh bound by bones.
It demands ownership over your soul -
It's your only remedy.
Love is a manipulation.
I hope you feel my pain one day too.

Oliwia Swierzcek (15)
Murray Park Community School, Mickleover

Insect Body

Some people think that insects don't mean a lot,
But this isn't entirely true.
I'll show you why.
With a rhythm to show,
How insects are loyal and true.

Insects are linked to our bodies alike.
By more than what you think.
If you allow the simple explanation.
To make you aware, I will do.

Surprisingly the bee comes first,
The busiest ones in fact.
It plays the part of the stomach for us,
By the pollen it brings back.

Another shock, the fly is heart.
'The filthy nasty thing'
They didn't deserve the squish,
Nor squash,
By less than you really think.

Finally and last of all,
The wriggly worm arrives.
The soul of the soil,
Creator of compost
It all ties in at last.

So to say as far as morals go,
I hope that this little rhyme has shown,
That insects do as insects are,
And that's what they're here to do.

Bella Matassa (13)
Murray Park Community School, Mickleover

Just Be You

No matter how many times you get put down or discriminated
it's alright to cry and not forget all the lies,
no matter how much you get put down you need to try to rise
everyone has that one thing that they hate about themselves
no matter if you are black or white you still matter
everyone has their own dream job
you can be a doctor a singer
you can be a rapper
just know you are extraordinary for being you
who would have ever known that me and you are so similar and different at the same time
I know we all go through rough times sometimes
we all get bullied and put down but we all are beautiful in our own way
and everyone loves me and you in every single way.
Even if people say it's not true throw their thoughts away
and listen to me you are extraordinary for being you.

Kacey Moon (12)
Murray Park Community School, Mickleover

Is Life Fair?

How can we just sell humans,
Like an object on the street?
How is human trafficking okay?
Imagine if they were people getting 'sold',
Imagine if they had no clean food or water,
Imagine if they were girls with no education,
Is that fair?
Why should they be these poor, helpless victims,
Who go through life without a reason -
No education, no parents, no food or water,
No toilets, no freedom,
All this because of someone's colour, age,
Race, background, gender, ethnicity -
Or just their religion?
Why would you do that?
Maybe people need to look at life in a positive way,
With positive thoughts,
Maybe that is fair.

Jay Sran (12)
Murray Park Community School, Mickleover

Dreams

Let's soar above the mountains
And dance beneath the stars
Live the life we are made for
Not just sitting in cars

We are made for greater things
Not all understand
The chances to touch the future
And to live in our lands

Some things are left to dream
And wishes in your heart
Yet knowing there's something bigger
That are all a part

So let the dream continue
And kindle well the fire
To push us on towards greatness
That we all should aspire.

Isabella Landless (12)
Murray Park Community School, Mickleover

What Is It?

It's just a rock
Is it?
The sun appears and the kaleidoscope of colours springs from the depths,
Chasing, weaving, screaming out for my attention.
Golds, blues greens transforming the surface to an incandescent sheen.
Beauty, the euphoric joy that radiates out.

It's just a rock
Is it?
My eyes are drawn to the mesmerising flow of colours,
Drawing me deeper and deeper,
Forgetting home, events and people,
Deeper and deeper into the universe's glow.

It's just a rock
Is it?
My soul is alive,
Transfixed on the undulating currents of the majesty of colour
I am one, at peace, I belong
Finally a home that accepts me, just me.

It's just as rock
Is it?
Clouds, only clouds can draw my soul back from its resting place,

Colours once so emotional and accepting flee
Drawn back into the dark depths waiting,
Always waiting.

It's just a rock
Is it?

Eowyn Tirion Vaughan (14)
Penglais School, Aberystwyth

Insecurities

Social media is very deceiving
Young girls with insecurities longing to be thin and perfect like all models
Using immense amount of filters to hide their flaws like freckles and scars
Longing for clear skin just like these influencers
But what those young girls don't see, don't understand, is that it's all a lie
Their idols use photoshop to be perfect
Filters to be perfect
They hide natural beauty so it's no longer natural anymore
Insecurities eating these innocent girls alive as they try their best to cover themselves up with baggy and oversized clothes
Not wearing what makes them happy because they are scared to be judged
It needs to stop
It's becoming an epidemic
Insecurities spreading and it's being ignored
We're beauty judged on social media for being ourselves
And quite frankly, it's not good!

Lottie Whitaker (13)
The Blyth Academy, Blyth

Human Nature

We worry about our planet.
We think it's going to die.
But we couldn't lay a finger on our planet if we tried.
The Earth has endured worse,
It doesn't feel too hurt.
The truth is we don't realise
What little threat we pose to Earth.
We overestimate ourselves -
How mankind's ego swells!
What we really should be worrying about
Is the threat we pose to ourselves.
We've created this crude system
Based on hate and greed.
Entitled tyrants sit on their thrones,
Others go without their basic needs.
Must there be someone
Who is better than the rest?
What determines who's superior?
What makes someone the best?
Is it their skin? Their gender?
Their family? Where they're from?
Is Mario superior to Sonic
Or Jerry better than Tom?
The fact that we believe

In this hierarchy of race,
If Martin Luther was still alive
It'd be a slap to his face.
But that's not the worst of it -
Oh no, no not at all!
The most disgusting action of mankind
Is the one that we call 'War'.
So many young soldiers
Will never live past their prime.
Evil men feel they have the right
To end a thousand lives.
So many people with their own stories,
With their family and their trade.
Those stories came to an abrupt end,
When one man said 'Invade'.
You should only ever fight
When you're fighting in defence,
To protect those you care for
From the ones you fight against.
So let's end this crude and unjust system
Based on hate and greed.
Let's forget, for a moment, about what we want
And think about what we need.
We need to see the light
And start a new rebirth.
Create a world of peace
Upon our good ol' Earth.

Bruno Cowan (13)
The Blyth Academy, Blyth

Hello Future Me

Hello future me
Don't hide in the shadows away from the world
The world can be a cruel and terrible place
But can also be a fun and great place
Hello future me
People can be cruel but can also be nice
Attempt to find that person
It will take weeks, months or even years
But you will find that special person
Hello future me
Always stay careful near people
But that doesn't mean to reject all people
Look, find and acquire that special person
Trust your family
Figure your identity
Expand your knowledge and don't repeat mistakes
Hello future me
Acknowledge your surroundings before it's too late
Explore the world
Go on vacation
Look at the Seven Wonders
Hello future me
Enjoy your life while you still have it
Go skydiving, surfing, fishing and bungee-jumping

Hello future me
Keep your soul strong
Get a good job
Not a job that spoils you but a job with good pay
Hello and goodbye future me.

Connor Pallister (13)
The Blyth Academy, Blyth

Passion

I stepped out into the buzzing atmosphere
I sat down and the gigantic roar engulfed my ears
The game kicked off
Pass, pass, pass
Players on the pitch were thrilling
Our team spirit started to melt
As we went 1-0 down
The crowd roared and roared to give encouragement to the players
The managers barked instructions onto the pitch
The ball smacked the post
The crowd roared louder and louder
As the team were working super hard
All of a sudden our number 7 picked up the ball
He ran and stepped over
He got past one
He got past another
Was something magical about to happen?
He cut inside
Skipped past another
He faked his first shot
He shot
The ball smashed against the back of the net
The crowd screamed, "Yes!"
We were back level

With five minutes to go
What a goal!

Harry Johnson (12)
The Blyth Academy, Blyth

How Do You Feel?

How do you feel?
How do you feel when people poke and prod and tear down your self-esteem?

How do you feel?
How do you feel when everyone points out your flaws
What you look like
How you act or feel
Or commenting on your weight?

How do you feel?
How do you feel when you see the perfect body
Or the perfect person online
The perfect body shape, clear skin
The flawless facial features?

But let me tell you
You are perfect
You are beautiful and you are the best person you can be

Everybody is different
And everybody is different
But that is what makes us a society
A planet
That is what makes us, us!

Whether you have clear skin, sparkly eyes, spots
A bigger nose, a smaller nose
Soft lips, dry lips.

Grace Murphy (13)
The Blyth Academy, Blyth

Sticks And Stones

Respect, we all deserve it
But if time flies by and the clouds in the sky
Just stop moving and all life freezes
What would you do?
If you're being put down or you are in distress
And nobody is around to help carry you
You are alone
But one thing's for sure
No one can get in your way
To stop you from saying hey
No one is stopping you from finding your voice and standing strong
Because if you weren't here now
You would already be gone
Left vulnerable for another time
For the predator to attack
And push you back
But since you're still here
Fasten an ear to the words you speak
Because these are the most important of them all
Sticks and stones may break your bones
But names will never hurt you.

Dillan Hunter (13)
The Blyth Academy, Blyth

Thanks For Everything You Do

You gave me life
You helped me when I was stuck like a knot on a rope
And for that I want to thank you
You gave me power and strength
You listened to my problems
You always inspired me each and every day
I faced the unexpected
It's been the hardest of years
But I powered on thanks to you
I think I would have been driven up the wall
If you ever went away
It can only go on from here with our new life in Cramlington
But the one thing I ask
However bad it may seem and even though the truth may sting
I will reach out to you every day
So keep a smile on your face
Because I love you
So all I ask is that you hold on tight when I go
As when I leave you
It may hurt
But eventually, we will part.

Grace Brown (12)
The Blyth Academy, Blyth

Empowerment

Flowers are blooming.
My heart is choosing.
As the sun directs me to my place,
Reminding me of the challenges I faced,
I lay on a tree,
Something fell on me,
An apple?
Oh how odd it seemed,
Showing all its insecurities,
That is what I dreamed,
To present all my impurities,
The tears we cry,
Make us lose all pride,
Words feel like bricks,
People feeding us all these tricks,
Lies fill our hearts,
Stabbing us like poison darts,
No one is the same,
So no one should go through the pain,
No one feels safe,
In all this tight space,
Everyone is different,
So give them a compliment,
Everyone can love who they want,
No one should cover that with a font.

Kayda Cole (12)
The Blyth Academy, Blyth

Taking Our Start

The wind in the air
The breeze in our heart
When the time is right
We all get a start
Strength in the air
Strength in our heart
When the time is right
We all get a start
The ground we step on
The hope in the sky
All these things can help us fly
Help us reach the sky
When the world just tears us apart
All these things can give us a start
But what do we do when we get this big start
Will you take it
Or let the world tear you down?
The time is now
To take that start
Just raise your head
With the wind in the air
And breeze in your heart
The time is now
To take a start.

Alfie Sloan (13)
The Blyth Academy, Blyth

Music Gets Me

You listened to my problems of any length
Even though you're just a song
You always give me advice and help me to be the best
Even though life was delayed
All I did was lay silent and listen to you play
Can I just say thank you all in all
Dear future me
I ask of you one thing
Please let music guide you along the way
Music is home
Trust it with life forever
It gives you hope
Smile so proudly and don't be afraid to admit how you feel
Even if the truth must sting
Music has your back
Always and forever
Don't let go of your shimmer
Be happy behind the mask too!

Niomi Carr (13)
The Blyth Academy, Blyth

Save Ukraine

We are gifted with friends
We are gifted with family
We receive strength
We get our issues solved of any length

But we now need to help
We need to save Ukraine from its cries and yelps
We need to save Ukraine like family or friends

Now is the perfect time to listen
Now we try and help Ukraine glisten
Now we need to take them in as family and friends
Now we need to help them through their tragedies

They now need our dignity
They now need our wealth
They now want support against the Russian army
They now need a family to hold.

Connor Angus (12)
The Blyth Academy, Blyth

The Covid Pandemic

The year of 2020
"We are all in the same boat!'" most say
But me, I disagree
So many different boats
Upon this stormy sea

The year of 2020
Some speed along in electric boats
Rushing to be let free
Just them at sea
Trying to stay afloat

The year of 2020
Some struggle on battleships
Fighting the good fight
Endlessly preparing
But nothing gets right

The year of 2020
It's been the hardest of years
We've tried to stay on the same boat
To support each other
And stay at port.

Abbie Humphreys (13)
The Blyth Academy, Blyth

Believe

Keep going, no matter how bad things may seem
Even in the dark there will always be a light beam

Keep going, even if you feel as grey as the sky
Even in the saddest moments there will not be a reason to cry

Keep going, even in the meanest of moments
Even in the bad times there will always be the greenest of fields on your doorstep

Keep going, even if you don't want to get out of bed
Even in the most boring of times, you have to look ahead

There is only one thing to fear in life
When you don't bring yourself to believe.

Lee Humble (13)
The Blyth Academy, Blyth

Bars Of Justice

Races, they don't matter
And yet people still make a fuss
Or a chatter
About skin colours
Or if people are thinner
Or fuller

Races, they don't matter
So why does the world lock them up?
So why do we care
If our views are important
But are not to share?

Races, they don't matter
But these bars are blocking us
Blocking our views on society
Blocking our trust

So free our views
Free our opinions
And free us
From these bars of justice.

Leona Goulding (12)
The Blyth Academy, Blyth

To Those In Ukraine

To those who live in Ukraine
To those who suffer endless slaughter
I have a message for those in pain
To the people who are as precious as a daughter

To those who live in Ukraine
To those who dream of a place to build
Blood's pouring like an endless rain
Don't forget, you're the heart of the world

To those who live in Ukraine
One day you will all be safe in your beds
One day you will be released from this pain
One day you will be free from dread.

Kain Waugh (12)
The Blyth Academy, Blyth

Max Verstappen

Every Sunday I will wait for your arrival
Whether it's sunshine, rain or snow
I sit there waiting for the words
It's light out and away we go

Max Verstappen; seemingly fearless
Doing whatever it takes
Even the slightest of errors
Could leave to the biggest of mistakes

Crossing the finish for a race win
Achieving every rookie's dream
An army of fans hurdling the barricades
In Spain 2016 Max Verstappen broke records with ease.

Josh Walton (12)
The Blyth Academy, Blyth

A Very Random Poem

In this poem I will ramble
For my brain is in a shamble
I want to feel brave but
It's just a wave of stupidity

I want to feel like I'm as large
As a king but all my achievements are a mirage
I just want to play games
But I crave fame

Even though I know I can do better
Life is like a simple letter
It may look bland on the outside
But it is just as great as I can imagine
So as I sit on the side I know I'm grand!

Harry Lawson (13)
The Blyth Academy, Blyth

Empowered To Be Me

E mpowerment is not just a word
M any people don't know the true meaning
P eople who take no notice of what they have in this world
O ften fail to believe in themselves
W e all take our self-control for granted
E veryone is able to take power
R eading, writing, you control yourself
E veryone is able to take control
D on't take advantage of the power... you never know
when you might lose it.

Hannah Rowe (12)
The Blyth Academy, Blyth

The Freedom Of Music

M usic, it makes me feel free and above and empowered to follow my dreams
U sing different sounds, tunes and each song I listen to has a meaning
S inging song lyrics that have purpose and a feeling
I listen to music because it fills me with freedom and I can relate to certain songs
C an you make this feeling a reality? With music you can show your feelings without having to express them. I feel free when listening to music.

Brooke McQuinn (13)
The Blyth Academy, Blyth

Dear Future Me

Dear future me
We feel the unexpected
We faced whatever came our way
We perfected what could be perfected
Letting nothing stand in our way

Dear future me
All I ask of you
Is to ask of you
Is to stay strong
The truth may sting
But always see it through

Dear future me
It has been tough
Sometimes have rough
But all I ask of you
Is remember to smile
And always stay strong.

Eoin Houghton
The Blyth Academy, Blyth

What Have We Done?

Dear future us
We have faced the unexpected
During the last few years
We have tried to perfect what we could have perfected
It was hard for all
But we fought the good fight
Dear future us
The person who helped us
And for that
For everything
I want to say thank you
I want to say to the bullies/haters
Stop
You're ruining people's lives
We want a happy world!

Megan Hedley-George (11)
The Blyth Academy, Blyth

Now Or Never

To everyone that wants to take the chance
It's now or never
You can do what you want
Not what others want

To everyone that wants to fulfil their dreams
It's now or never
Take the chance and make something good of it

What do you want to do?
A doctor, a police officer or even an athlete?
Well, make it from a reality to a future
It's now or never.

Mitchell Arnold (13)
The Blyth Academy, Blyth

The Boxer

With every high there is a low
With every punch there is a blow
Like a boxer I will not leave the ring
Until I can raise my arms in victory
Blood and sweat may drip down
But I will always stand my ground
Like Rocky I will make another round
I will battle the years
Wipe my tears and conquer my fears
I may end up black and blue
At least I know I always stayed true!

Stella Anderson (12)
The Blyth Academy, Blyth

Dear Future Me

Dear future me
Believe in yourself
And embrace every day

Dear future me
Remember happiness is a praise
And never forget that family is a gift

Dear future me
Think about the good times, forget about the bad
Never give up and follow your dreams

Dear future me
I ask of you one thing
Reach out to family and friends, they love you.

Grace Stoker (12)
The Blyth Academy, Blyth

What Makes You... You?

The key question is what makes you... you?
Think about it
You have lived for so long and you don't even know yourself

You have let those awful words get to you
And now you don't know yourself

So what makes you... you?
Is it that you love animals, a movie or anything?
Something that makes you different!

What makes you... you?

Elise James (12)
The Blyth Academy, Blyth

Music To Me

Music to me can be loud
Like thunder in my head
Music to me can be soft
That draws me to bed
Music to me is strong

Music to me makes me feel
Like I can do no wrong

Music to me makes a better tomorrow
Or makes you full of sorrow
Music to me can make a difference

Music to me is when you see
Who you really are.

Kendal Davison (13)
The Blyth Academy, Blyth

The Poem Of Determination

D on't give up
E ncouragement
T ry your hardest
E mpower yourself
R esilience
M ake it happen
I ndependence
N ever quit on your dreams
A lways power through
T ake that chance
I nitiative
O pportunities
N ow it's your time to shine.

Junior Gooch (13)
The Blyth Academy, Blyth

Positivity Is Key

Be kind
To each other because it could cause
Pain emotionally and mentally
Otherwise people may not see
That factor of life
Life is meant to be positive
Today, tomorrow and yesterday can be changed
I have made life positive for other people
Very more people can do that too
Everything you say can change a life.

Mollie-Ann Hardy (12)
The Blyth Academy, Blyth

Tears

You gave me life
When I needed it the most
You brought me comfort
Even now you're a ghost

I miss making memories
I miss playing ball
I miss everything about you
I really miss it all

Saying goodbye to you
Was my worst ever fear
I wish it never happened
I wish that you were here.

Mason-Lee Scott (12)
The Blyth Academy, Blyth

Roses Are Red, Violets Are Blue

Roses are red, violets are blue
The human race is dying
The planet is too
We need to act now
Before it's too late
It's only a matter of time
Before the human race and endangered species go extinct!
Empower those that don't have power themselves
Act before all is lost.

Zak Barber (13)
The Blyth Academy, Blyth

Empowerment

E veryone should have power
M ore people should devour
P ushing the limits will help you succeed
O nly if you have too much power you'll greed
W e must push past the limits
E veryone should come together
R aising the happiness forever.

Aleesha Knox (13)
The Blyth Academy, Blyth

Change

I am the world
I give life
I give land

I am the world
I give sea
I give trees

I am the world
People take my creations
People take my world.

Sarah Dormand (13)
The Blyth Academy, Blyth

The Five Stages Of Grief

1: Denial
You fall to the ground and
Deny, deny, deny
Refuse to believe
"They can't just leave!"
And the pain starts to weigh you down

2: Anger
Anger makes you scream and let it all out
You shout and shout
Cry and cry
Until you can't any more

3: Bargaining
You ask yourself: 'What if?'
To make you feel better
And scenarios swim around in your head

4: Depression
Your heart feels empty
Like a vacuum inside you

5: Acceptance
You finally accept what's happened.

Zofia Migel (11)
The Henry Box School, Witney

Ukraine

Help them,
You're the only one,
Be their light in the sky,
Like the sun.

Help them,
We can't wait anymore,
We have to chase those bullies,
Out of the door.

Please Boris Johnson,
They'll ruin the Earth,
The Russians are invading,
Ukraine's turf.

Not one person can do something,
We have to unite,
If we do something,
You might be able to sleep well tonight.

Stop Priti Patel, don't send them home,
They need our help,
If you sent them
Then in your sleep, you will hear them yelp.

We all need
To play our part
'Cause after all
We all have a heart.

Gemma Hardie (12)
The Henry Box School, Witney

What Have We Done?

Look at the Earth and see what we have done,
Chopping down trees, now animals' homes are gone.
Slowly animals are becoming extinct,
If you love cats then save the lynx.

The Tasmanian tiger and great auk,
The woolly mammoth and the Spix's macaw
All these animals gone forever
Will you see them again?
No, never!

Climate change is causing droughts
Which is making wildfires, that's no doubt
Everything that's happening is so strange
If you want to make a difference, then make a change.

Emma Smith (13)
The Henry Box School, Witney

The Earth's Call

Polar bears lose their prey
As the Arctic's ice melts away
Global temperatures are rising
Over twice as much but it is not surprising
Fossil fuels, plastic pollution
We need to find a solution
Transportation and deforestation
Eliminate our vacillation
Compensate for our past contributions
And protect our Earth from further complications.

Melissa Li (13)
The Henry Box School, Witney

It

It controlled her
It took over her
She knew that
She knew it would end her
Everyone knew it
Nothing could treat it
Therapists, doctors
She tried them all
They thought it was cool
It was drowning her in a pool
Until the final day
Of her life
She shut her eyes
And said goodnight.

Jessica Miller (11)
The Henry Box School, Witney

Being Me

Being me can be easy yet so rough
I walk with the sun over me
When the sun leans over to smile at me
I feel so free
Being me is easy
Being me feels free
I no longer see dark alleys
The sun brightens them for me
I'm floating on clouds
Not a worry in me because the sun shines over me
With such ecstasy, what could bother me?

The jealous clouds don't like the sun
The jealous clouds don't like the sun
The jealous clouds can't see
The sun making me happy
So the bitter clouds start a riot
They darken the sun's light
They block over the sun
Now the clouds rain over me
Being me is so rough when the clouds spread their disease
Now I wait desperately
Longing for the sun to see me
So I can get back to being me.

Kyla Olopade (14)
Trinity School, Lee

The Life Of A Mango Tree

Forest

A vibrant tide of stagnant evergreen
A pastoral battlefront of savagery and retribution
Like mankind's damned reality
I'm the light that declines the repugnant evil
My grateful quintessence is one of many

Mango tree

My physique is an erect but acclaimed art
My trunk courses like the stream of fluid life regurgitating this helpless rock of its everlasting possibility
My body borders being that of which is a vast tropical disease of this world
My hair shines like the graceful luminescence of the world's first morning
My cream-pink petal dress reminds me of beauty and the world's floral landscape

Mango

My spawn is an unsymmetrical test to the tongues of the self-righteous fleshy beings
Those bipedal ravagers seek the redeeming purifying radiance of its skin
The atmospheric vibrancy like the bountiful harvest of pitiful men
But its sweetness like the reawakening of the perpetual bond between men and beast

Although the seed of the ever-preserved lurks within

Ants

The harmony and amalgamation of synchronisation and dominance reigned supreme in the eyes of the diligent
The striving nation of represented boundless blind faith and power leads to eternal chaos
Anarchy, democracy, tyranny
The bittersweet chains of the intelligent man and insect alike
Not prohibited by the sense that conformed this world and waging in the hands of inevitable fate
Like humans
Pilgrims of revelation, declaration, transformation
War and self-proclaimed insightfulness and enlightenment are such a global symphony

One year later

A nondescript tide of dormant evergreen
Lay waste by the feral man and its ideology
Apparatus at hand
Man and machine: harbingers of pure havoc
Yet only one naughty being will reign supreme in the end
Or peace could be a glorious hymn sung in a universal lament
Change, the compass of fate, the continuous alternating allurement of nature.

Jayden Bediako (12)
Trinity School, Lee

No Pain, No Gain

I'd made my plans on a Friday's eve for the coming weekend
To get some sleep
On the weekend I'd be relieved,
No school, no alarm clock,
Just me feeling at ease.
I could see my friends, go to the park
And take out my art book and have a look.
As I was making my plans for the weekend ahead
I heard my mum's footsteps from behind my bed.
She made the announcement, I filled with dread
"I'm doing your hair this weekend, so early out of bed!"
Paranoia, anger and gloom filled my room
I didn't dare to ask what day, all I knew was it would be mundane
My sister laughed, knowing my fear
As she uttered, "A few more years!"
I know what she meant
But it didn't help
The date had been given and so had my fate
I wondered if any of my mates experienced this hate.
Morning arrived, the sun was out
All I could think about was would my mum shout
"Get the towel, get the comb, let's do your hair!"
I stayed in bed imagining I wasn't there.
Sleep paralysis devoured my body
Leaving a hopeless sensation as I couldn't run.

The scene was set
Water was dropping from my forehead.
Fingers rubbing, attacking my scalp
Bubbles foaming, cleansing my hair.
How I wished I was not there!
The wash was completed, now to blowdry
My Afro had shrunk and was about to fry.
The knots were many, the water had made it frizzy and dense,
The pulling and tugging was intense.
Next was parting and oiling and it cooled my brain.
My mum's fingers were weaving through my hair, then I heard her say
"One more left and you can play!"
It had been two hours, my hair smelt like flowers
Knowing it was coming to an end
I couldn't bend
Now I could go on Instagram and begin to trend.
I looked in the mirror, I was full of pride
My hair was shining and looking right.
Now it was done, I hugged my mum,
Saying a big thank you for all she had done.

Aaria Asafa (11)
Trinity School, Lee

The Time-Traveller Plan

A time traveller he was
Travelling across the universe
Through all time and space
He'd seen galaxies, suns, solar systems, planets
Old yet young
Wise yet foolish

He had seen so much
Some would say everything
But no, that all changed when he saw it
A tiny speck in the blackness of space
A miracle of life, a wonder
Unlike anything he had seen
So he raced quicker than he'd ever gone before
To the planet, the planet called Earth

He went, he saw, he listened
To the beautiful sound
Of birdsong and water
Rushing through the river
A cacophony of beauty

Again he travelled
This time through time
To the future of the Earth
Excited to see what it will become

However the sight that greeted him
Was not what he imagined
Death, yes nothing
Leafless trees, dark grey clouds
Was birdsong, no rivers, just nothing

Devastated he started his plan
With haste so it was not too late
Teaching humanity what to do
To save them, save the world

He worked tirelessly for what seemed like eternity
Never stopping
Until he was done

After he had done as much as he could
He went back to the future
To the one he tried to save
He stepped out into the new world and smiled

All the humans had to do was change
So he could hear the birdsong again.

Jacob Forgie (12)
Trinity School, Lee

Will Nature Win?

When I gaze upon the extravagant ecstasies of life
I get a great exhilaration
Though much of the world is disease and strife
My other parts undergo a development acceleration
Rolling hills of trees can stretch for miles long
Whilst perched atop the smallest twig
Birds tweet out their song
Or to raging ocean storms - raw uncontrolled power
Mountains of heaving water, free of ships and oil rigs
Always changing and flowing, always looking to devour
Yet despite all this scenery, much of it is destroyed
And due to such, the world becomes paranoid
Swaths of untouched greenery
Burnt mercilessly to the ground
All this wonderful scenery
Gone with not a trace to be found
As man lays waste to nature's Eden
We must keep our minds diligent
Or we will deviate
None of us are innocent
So we must all start to create
A new way forward in which
Nature is our neighbour
Destructive habits need to switch
To win our planet's favour

And to save our dying host
Abide to nature's laws
Attend to your past
And let us end this annoying war.

Zeke Coventry (12)
Trinity School, Lee

Don't Tell Me

Discrimination is fine
Don't tell me
Being different isn't a crime
Stereotypes are all true
Don't tell me
Current mindset is cruel
Foreigners can't come in
Don't tell me
There's a new way to think
We should all be the same
Don't tell me
Dark skin isn't to blame
Muslims are all terrorists
Don't tell me
Every religion has extremists
Homosexuals should be banned
Don't tell me
Love can be between more than woman and man
Women are supposed to be paid less
Don't tell me
Men don't know best
It's okay the lower class suffer more
Don't tell me
The rich don't know the score
This is the finished story

Don't tell me
Diversity is glory
(Now read upwards.)

Fettan Khemiri (12)
Trinity School, Lee

Alternate Universe

Life pulls us apart,
leaving us to fix ourselves together.
We struggle every day,
feeling like it won't get better.
Never knowing if the sadness will go.
Deeper and deeper in the thoughts we go.

There is an alternate universe we ought to go.
In this alternate universe life put us back together.
Every day seems to get better.
Deeper and deeper in the universe we go,
we step upon a pointy stone.

Pain and confusion all floods in.
All the happiness and glee leaves our skin.
Deeper and deeper in the alternate universe we go.
Life is not where we ought to go.
Leaving us to fix ourselves together,
never knowing if it will ever get better.

Lauren-Kaye Ward (15)
Trinity School, Lee

Competitions

In a world of competitions
We live with different aspirations about the competition
Some remain in tension
But we should enjoy it
Let me mention
Competition is not about the pressure
But to realise our treasure
To forget every leisure
Taking the effective
Improving measures
Everyone wants to be a winner as they hate to be a failure
But the necessary thing is to be the competitor
Instead of the prize
Who is interested to be stronger
Important thing to participate without thinking about our talents rare
Competition opens a new gate to express our talents and not our fate.

Leila Boukhari (15)
Trinity School, Lee

Oh Our World

Oh our world
A place filled with darkness, hatred and industries
Inside the sexist
Inside the racist
Sometimes I wonder where the hope is
But as I see
The world as an orange
The outside filled with bumps and bruises
Time by time
The orange opens up
Bruises easing just like us humans making progress
Sometimes even having to protest
But please my fellow comrades
Help us and help yourself
Help everyone but most importantly
Help our world...
A place filled with joy and happiness.

Oluwanifemi Ajimobi (12)
Trinity School, Lee

The Journey

I am wounded by darkness
Trapped behind chains of misery
Bound by the flashbacks of history
I am drowned
Drowned by the suffocating harsh voices
'You're not good enough
'Just die!'
'Worthless'
Dark deep eyes stare at me from above
Emotionless, judgemental eyes stare at me with no love
But then there's light
A crack in the endless amount of walls
It is calling to me
Awaiting a new journey
Awaiting a new destiny
Finally, finally I am free.

Shane Grant (11)
Trinity School, Lee

School

It's our final year of Year 11
By the end of it I will be sixteen
The pupils will know the school the best
The one who has taken every test
The ones that know the routines and rules
The ones ready to leave for sixth form
Now that we are in Year 12
New things will be added to our intelligence
Difficult calculations, forms of writing
Each term will be exciting
We come as children
But leave as young adults
To a whole new world.

Aleem Mansaray (12)
Trinity School, Lee

Just Remember

If I could fly
I'd touch the sky
I would never cry
Unless someone died
If you were me
What would you be?
A footballer? A basketballer?
Be what you believe
Your imagination can go as far as the eye can see
So if someone tells you you can't do it
Just remember, believe!
No matter how many times you get knocked down
Get back up and just remember
Never give up...

Giovanni Josiah-Taylor (12)
Trinity School, Lee

YoungWriters
Est. 1991

YOUNG WRITERS INFORMATION

We hope you have enjoyed reading this book – and that you will continue to in the coming years.

If you're the parent or family member of an enthusiastic poet or story writer, do visit our website **www.youngwriters.co.uk/subscribe** and sign up to receive news, competitions, writing challenges and tips, activities and much, much more! There's lots to keep budding writers motivated!

If you would like to order further copies of this book, or any of our other titles, then please give us a call or order via your online account.

Young Writers
Remus House
Coltsfoot Drive
Peterborough
PE2 9BF
(01733) 890066
info@youngwriters.co.uk

Join in the conversation!
Tips, news, giveaways and much more!

YoungWritersUK YoungWritersCW youngwriterscw